TUBA TUNE RAGTIME

George Baker

Exclusively Distributed by
HAL•LEONARD

www.FredBock.com

to the Prothro and Yeager families - Wichita Falls, Texas

TUBA TUNE RAGTIME

Organ Solo

Music by
GEORGE BAKER

8

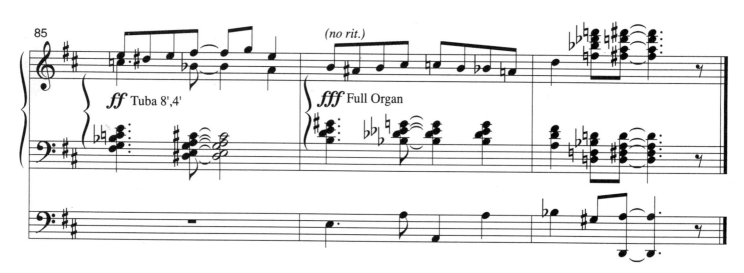

Exclusively Distributed By

HAL•LEONARD®
CORPORATION

7777 W. BLUEMOUND RD. P.O. BOX 13819 MILWAUKEE, WI 53213

08739797 Tuba Tune Ragtime JG0719 Organ $7.95

0 73999 39797 0